香港國際詩歌之夜 2017
INTERNATIONAL POETRY NIGHTS IN HONG KONG

編輯 Editors

北島 Bei Dao

柯夏智 Lucas Klein

宋子江 Chris Song

公路旁的紅罌粟

林舜玲

POPPIES BY THE MOTORWAY

AGNES S.L. LAM

《公路旁的紅罌粟》
林舜玲 著

封面影像：北島

國際統一書號 (ISBN)：978-988-237-041-8

出版：中文大學出版社
香港 新界 沙田・香港中文大學
傳真：+852 2603 7355
電郵：cup@cuhk.edu.hk
網址：www.chineseupress.com

Poppies by the Motorway
By Agnes S.L. Lam

Cover Image: Bei Dao

ISBN: 978-988-237-041-8

Published by The Chinese University Press
The Chinese University of Hong Kong
Sha Tin, N.T., Hong Kong
Fax: +852 2603 7355
E-mail: cup@cuhk.edu.hk
Website: www.chineseupress.com

Printed in Hong Kong

目錄 Contents

Acknowledgements

Some of the poems first appeared in various publications:

Lam, A. (2010). "White Orchids on Concrete." *Muse 42*, 93.

Lam, A. (2014). "Time to Go." *Asiatic 8*(2), 263–264.

Lam, A. (2016). "The Gate of Heaven." In J. J. Morales, T. Ho, D. McKirdy and G. Muñoz (Eds.), *Quixotica: Poems East of La Mancha* (pp. 46–47). Hong Kong: Chameleon Press.

Lam, A. (2017). "Somewhere Else." *Wasafiri 32*(1), Issue 89, available online www.tandfonline.com/10.1080/02690055.2017.1252094

The kind permission to reprint and translate them is gratefully acknowledged.

林舜玲

Agnes S.L. Lam

中文翻譯：陳嘉恩

White Orchids on Concrete

Waking on my third morning
in Balay Internasyonal, I found
white orchids on the concrete wall,

six or seven of them growing
without stems or leaves or roots,
arched above the foot of my bed.

"What do they mean?" I wondered
throughout my Saturday outing
in Ayala with my Filipino friend,

sauntering through the Greenbelts
of yuppie pubs, designers' republic,
bamboo gardens with carp in the ponds…

At the museum, we walked through millennia
of Filipino history – the Chinese, the Muslims,
the Spanish, the Americans, the Japanese,

and finally the Filipinos – the same old story
played out almost to a cue on different soils
in Asia. What happened five centuries ago,

even one century before, could be forgiven,
if not forgotten. But twenty-odd years ago,
my Filipino sister was not yet thirty when

she joined millions on the streets soon after
I saw on television in America the murder of
Ninoy Aquino stepping off the plane in Manila.

As we stood among the sea of faces on film
in the museum, tears came. And I understood
what the white orchids on concrete meant.

22 February 2010, the anniversary of the People Power Revolution, University of the Philippines Balay Internasyonal, for Lily Rose

混凝土上的白蘭花

第三天早上醒來
於國際賓館，我看見
混凝土牆上的白蘭花

長有六七株
沒有莖或葉或根，
拱立在我的床腳之上。

「它們是甚麼意思？」我想知道，
星期六郊遊時一直想。
在愛雅拉，我跟隨菲律賓朋友

漫步綠化帶
串連優皮酒吧、設計師共和國
竹子園裏的池塘有鯉魚……

博物館內，我們穿越了一千年的
菲律賓歷史——華人、穆斯林、
西班牙人、美國人、日本人，

還有菲律賓人—— 一樣的老故事，
不同的土壤上，仿如按照提示演出
於亞洲。五個世紀前發生過的事情，

甚至一世紀前發生過的，都可以被原諒，
如果沒有被人遺忘。可是二十多年前，
我的菲律賓姐妹還不到三十歲，當時

她隨百萬民眾上街，不久之前，
我在美國電視看見尼諾·阿基諾
在馬尼拉甫下機，即遭殺害。

影片中人臉如海，我們站在中間
在博物館裏，流下淚來。我明白了
混凝土上的白蘭花是甚麼意思。

2010年2月22日，人民力量革命週年紀念，
菲律賓大學國際賓館，獻給Lily Rose

Time to Go

1967 –
we stayed put at home as
there were bombs in the streets.

1989 –
the smell of blood afar,
we all marched down Queensway.

2014 –
for a month and more days,
you have camped on the roads.

You have spoken your mind.
We have heard every word.
Even those who didn't care
now watch the news daily.

So try to listen please
to voices not your own.
To prison or to death
is not the only way.

Move to Tamar Park if
you still want to protest.
Or form your own party
to get into LegCo.

It's not the traffic jams.
It's not the business lost.
We just want to leave you
a place you can call home.

Time to go home, my friends.
It is still not too late.
No one would laugh at you.
We were all there before.

One fine day some winter,
you will walk down the streets,
feel the sun on your face.

In your mind, you may still
see the tents and your friends,

the mobile lights at night…

but you may wonder where
did all the hatred go,
what dreams were really dreamt…

31 October 2014, the 34th day of Occupy Central,
Admiralty

是時候走了

1967年——
我們安守家中，
因為街上有炸彈。

1989年——
遠方飄來血腥，
我們所有人遊行到金鐘道。

2014年——
一個月再多數天，
你在馬路上紮營。

你說出了你的心聲，
我們每個字都聽見了。
再漠不關心的人，
現在每天都看新聞。

所以，請細心聆聽
不屬於你自己的聲音。
監獄或者死亡
不是唯一的出路。

移師添馬艦去，假如
你還想抗議，
或組成你自己的政黨，
進軍立法會。

堵車不要緊，
丟了生意不要緊，
我們只想留給你
一個你可以喊一聲「家」的地方。

是時候回家了，我的朋友，
現在還不算太遲。
沒有人會取笑你，
我們都在那裏待過。

在晴朗的一天，某個冬天，
你會走在街上，
感到太陽曬在臉上。

你在心中，可能依然
看見帳篷和你的友伴，
夜裏手機的燈光……

可是你或會感到疑惑，
仇恨到哪裏去了，
夢裏到底夢見甚麼……

2014年10月31日，「佔領中環」第34天，金鐘

Somewhere Else

It happens somewhere else –
Tunisia, Egypt, Ukraine…
miles away on another continent.

We never understood how
within a week, a month,
a whole city could collapse.

It happens somewhere else –
Delhi, Bangkok, Manila…
streets full of angry people.

We never worried about
our city – so rich, so safe,
so free, so sensible…

It happens somewhere else –
it would not happen here,
we thought, but it has.

In this city now divided
at home, at school, at work,
even without death or riots,

we can only watch and pray
as we did when it happened
somewhere else far far away…

8 November 2014, the 42nd day of Occupy Central,
Café Landmark

別的地方

它發生於別的地方——
突尼西亞、埃及、烏克蘭……
數千哩外，在別的大陸。

我們永遠不明白為甚麼
一週之間，一個月之間，
整座城市會倒塌。

它發生於別的地方——
德里、曼谷、馬尼拉……
街上滿是憤怒的人們。

我們永遠不擔心
我們的城市——這麼富庶，這麼安全，
這麼自由，這麼理智……

它發生於別的地方——
卻不會在這裏發生，
我們曾經以為，可它的確發生了。

這個城市如今分裂了，
家裏、學校裏、公司裏，
即使沒有命案或騷亂，

我們只可以觀望和祈禱，
之前我們也這樣做，當它發生於
別的地方，遠遠之外……

2014年11月8日，「佔領中環」第42日，置地咖啡店

Poppies by the Motorway

You cannot touch them.
You cannot take clear photos of them.
They seem to grow only by the motorway in the wild.

Remembering the dead.
Remembering the war, the turmoil after.
Not to be found in the city centres where tourists
lunch on sidewalks.

The same red as the coat my Polish friend left.
On a stone bench under a tree by the Zakopane
post office in the mountains.
No one would take it.

The rain soaks it wet.
The sun dries it, time after time, season after season.
No one would take it, thinking the owner would come back.

Waiting to belong...

4 June 2014, on the road to Torun, for Beata

公路旁的紅罌粟

你不可以觸摸它們，
你不可以替它們拍清楚的照片，
它們似乎只會野生在公路旁。

惦記著死者，
惦記著戰爭、之後的動亂。
遊客在行人道上午餐的市中心，不會找到

同一抹紅色，好比我的波蘭朋友留下的外套，
在山中扎科柏內郵局旁樹下的石長凳上，
沒有人會拿走。

雨水弄濕它，
太陽曬乾它，一次又一次，一季復一季，
沒有人會拿走，想著物主將會回來。

等待屬於……

2014年6月4日，往托倫的路上，獻給Beata

Black Swan

On the way to Kotor
in Montenegro,

we passed by
an expanse of water,

mountains and cliffs
all around,

a small island
in the centre.

On the island,
a solitary palace.

The mist was floating
on the water,

forbidding strangers
to intrude…

A fairy tale setting,
a fairy tale ending

to life,
even if

the black swan
is lurking

in the fog,
ready to seduce

anyone –
man or woman…

25 December 2012, on the way to Kotor in Montenegro

黑天鵝

往科托爾的路上
在黑山

我們途經
一片廣漠的水、

山巒和懸崖，
面面環繞

一個小島
在中央。

小島上，
一座孤獨的宮殿。

薄霧漂浮
在水上，

禁止陌生人
闖進……

童話的場景
童話的結局，

那是屬於生命的，
縱有

黑天鵝
潛伏

濃霧中，
準備引誘

任何人——
男人或女人……

2012年12月25日，在黑山，往科托爾的路上

Pythons Crossing the Road

Eleven days before Christmas,
a Burmese python in her fifties
was crossing Castle Peak Road.

Weak eyes on her small head,
her four-metre-long body
bloated with roast geese,
she could only inch her way.

Someone spotted her
and the police came.
The snake-catcher waited till
she crawled onto the grass,
taped her mouth,
put two sacks over her
and carried her off
with three policemen
to care at Kadoorie.

Three months earlier,
another two-metre python
crossing Repulse Bay Road was
run over by a car. It crept

onto the pavement to die,
its age and sex unreported.

Long long time ago,
after Satan tempted Eve
in the guise of a snake,
God had forewarned,
"I shall put enmity
between her seed
and your seed.
He shall bruise your head.
You shall bruise his heel."

Is that why
most of us fear snakes
though it is said
they seldom bite
unless harassed?

Those two pythons
were not colourful.
But there are others –
the green bamboo viper

with diamonds down its back,
the milk snake with bands
of red and black on white,
the mystic turquoise snake
sparkling in moonlight,
the humble grass snake
slender as a branch…

Snakes come in a range of
colours, sizes and patterns –
almost like flowers.

If Satan had chosen
to take the form of
a flower in Eden,
would we now fear flowers

and give baby snakes
tied with matching ribbons
on Valentine's Day instead?

14 December 2016, Vantage Park

蟒蛇過路

聖誕前十一天，
一尾約五十歲的緬甸蟒蛇，
正在橫過青山道。

她的小頭上雙目無光，
四米長的身體
遭燒鵝撐脹了，
她只能寸進。

有人看見她，
然後警察來了。
捕蛇員伺機而動，等到
她爬入草叢，
用膠布封住她的口，
放兩個沙包壓著她
把她帶走，
三位警察
送她到嘉道理農場受監護。

三個月後，
另一尾兩米長的蟒蛇
橫過淺水灣道時
遭車踐過，牠爬到

行人道上才死去，
歲數和性別沒有報導。

好久好久之前，
撒旦偽裝成蟒蛇
引誘夏娃，
神已經警告說：
「我要使她的後裔
和你的後裔
彼此為仇，
他要傷你的頭，
你也要傷他的腳跟。」

是不是因為如此，
我們都害怕蛇，
儘管據說
牠們不常咬人，
除非受到騷擾？

那兩尾蟒蛇
紋理不斑斕，
但看其他的蛇——

竹葉青蛇
尾巴鑲鑽，
奶蛇渾身白色，
環帶紅色和黑色，
神秘的土耳其石蛇
月光下閃閃發光，
謙虛的草蛇
纖纖如樹枝……

蛇的種類繁多，
顏色、大小和紋理不一 ——
幾乎媲美花卉。

假若撒旦選擇
在伊甸園
偽裝成花朵，
現在我們會不會害怕花朵，

把蛇的嬰兒當禮物，
繫上配色的絲帶，
慶祝情人節？

2016年12月14日，慧豪閣

Christmas Eve

My friends invited me
to help them decorate
the church for Christmas.

But that morning,
my washing machine
refused to work.

I was surprised
they could send someone
even on Christmas Eve.

A head of grey came
in a dark brown sweater,
a black down jacket,
a worn briefcase,
a bag of spare parts
with all his tools.

The old man took off
the back of the machine.
Then the top.
I saw its internal organs

through the glass
of the kitchen door.

He put a new brain board in
but it wouldn't revive.
He swapped another brain
for the knob to no avail.
He changed a third one
for the LCD. It lit up

but still wouldn't move.
He checked and rechecked
the tap, the tubing, the drain,
screwed and unscrewed,
squatting, bending,
waiting, hoping…

In between,
I asked if he wanted
a break for lunch,
a banana or water.
"No, thank you.
I'm not hungry."

After four hours,
sitting on the floor,
he finally looked up,
"Cannot be repaired.
Must go back
to the factory."

I smiled and said,
"It's okay. Thank you
for trying to help us."

What I really wanted to say
was, "I'm sorry my machine
didn't respond to your care.

Have you no place,
no one to hurry back to,
even on Christmas Eve?"

24 December 2015, Vantage Park

平安夜

我的朋友邀請我
幫助他們裝飾
教堂賀聖誕。

可是那天早上，
我的洗衣機
拒絕操作。

我很驚訝，
他們竟可派人
在平安夜過來。

一頭灰髮來了，
穿著深棕色的衛衣，
黑色羽絨外套，
破爛的公事包，
一袋子零配件，
還有他所有的工具。

老頭子拆下
洗衣機的背板，
接著機頂，
透過廚房門的

玻璃，
我看見機器的內臟。

他把新的腦板裝進去，
可機器沒有復蘇；
他給旋鈕換上
另一塊腦板，也不得要領；
他替液晶顯示屏
換上第三塊，燈亮起來了，

但機器還是不動。
他檢查了又檢查
水龍頭、喉管、排水管，
擰緊再擰開，
蹲著，彎著腰，
等待著，期盼著⋯⋯

期間，
我問他要不要
稍休吃午餐、
香蕉或開水，

「不用了，謝謝，
我不餓。」

四小時後，
他坐在地上，
終於抬頭看我：
「修不了，
必須回
工廠去。」

我笑笑說：
「不打緊，有勞你
嘗試幫我們的忙。」

其實我想說的
是：「對不起，我的洗衣機
辜負了你的照料。」

你沒有地方、
沒有人趕著去嗎？
這可是平安夜。

2015年12月24日，慧豪閣

A Conversation with My Body

My body,

I have had enough of you.
You are too demanding.
You need to eat,
a place to sleep.

I can't let you eat too much
or too little.
You have to eat just right
or I'll feel pain somewhere.

You cannot be too cold
or too hot.
Too cold, you get asthma.
Too hot, you get rashes.

I need to change your bedsheets,
clean your toilet, mop your floor,
wash your clothes, buy supplies,
report gas usage, pay maintenance…

You are so troublesome.
Yet countries go to war
to find food and shelter
for bodies like you!

But my spirit,

I offer you my eyes
as windows to your world
to help you tell distance,
smile to people you love.

My legs carry you to
climb the Sahara sands,
wander onto glaciers,
swirl with the auroras.

My ears let you listen
to the sounds of mountains,
the bellow of oceans,
the stars still in the night.

At home, I scent honey,
the steam of rice cooking,
the tinge of tomatoes,
the wet hair of babies.

My fingers type the thoughts
you wish to share. I am
the only one who stays
with you from birth to death…

9 May 2016, Vantage Park

與我的身體對話

我的身體：

我受夠了你，
你要求太多，
你要吃，
還要地方睡覺。

我不能讓你吃太多
或太少，
你得吃得剛好，
不然我某個部位就會疼。

你不可太冷
或太熱，
太冷，你會哮喘；
太熱，你長皮疹。

我要替你換床單、
清潔你的馬桶、掃你的地、
洗你的衣服、買用品、
報煤氣用量、付維修費用……

你真麻煩，
卻有國家打起仗來，
去找食物和居所
給你這樣的身體！

可是呀，我的靈魂，

我給你我的眼睛，
讓你的世界有窗子，
幫你辨別距離，
對你愛的人微笑。

我的腿帶你去
爬撒哈拉沙漠，
浪蕩冰川，
繞著極光轉圈。

我的耳朵讓你聽到
山峰的聲音、
海洋的咆哮、
靜夜的星星。

在家裏，我嗅到蜜糖、
煮飯的蒸氣、
西紅柿的味道、
嬰兒的濕髮。

我的手指打出你想分享的
思想，我是
唯一留下
陪你的人，從生到死⋯⋯

2016年5月9日，慧豪閣

Sparrow

Walking to the market,
I saw a sparrow
hopping after another
across the pavement.

It was not afraid
of me or other pedestrians.
If we had not been careful,
we could have squashed it.

Or perhaps
there was no greater work
than being able to follow
the other sparrow.

21 May 2013, Robinson Road

麻雀

走進市場裏，
我看見一隻麻雀
隨著另一隻跳行，
穿梭行人道。

牠不怕
我或其他行人，
我們一不小心，
可要把牠壓扁。

不過或許
沒有事情重要得過
可以跟隨
另一隻麻雀。

2013年5月21日，羅便臣道

The Gate of Heaven

The gate of heaven
must be really far away

from Earth
because through it, the music
of goodness, the water
of eternity will flow, the light
of life will shine so brightly that
if it's too near Earth,
it will engulf our night,
no one can sleep at all.

The gate of heaven
has to be far beyond.

If it isn't,
everyone will crowd
and clamour before it,
our evil and dirt
may seep into heaven.

It will become noisy,
sticky, smoky, smelly,
just from proximity.

For heaven to exist,
there has to be a chasm…

One day,
I hope to knock on
the gate of heaven.
I wonder how many
light years it will take
to get there. Perhaps
I will fly faster than light
through cosmic voids…

… to Eden on a remote planet
in another universe.

12 May 2012, Rodrigues Court

天國之門

天國之門
一定真的遠離

地球，
因為從這門，美好的
音樂、永恆的
流水會流過，生命的
光輝會閃得明亮，
假如這光輝太近地球，
盡會吞噬我們的夜，
無人能睡。

天國之門
必然在遠遠之外。

不然，
人人會擠擁
又叫囂在門外，
我們的邪惡和污垢
會滲入天國，

天國盡會變得吵嚷的、
黏黏的、煙煙的、臭臭的，
咫尺可聞。

天國若是存在，
它必須有一度鴻溝……

有一天，
我希望去叩一叩
天國之門。
我不知道要花上
多少光年
才去得到。也許
我會飛得比光快，
越過宇宙的空間……

……飛到別的宇宙裏
遙遠星球上的伊甸園。

2012年5月12日，羅理基閣

林舜玲（香港），曾負笈新加坡及美國留學。她前任香港大學教授，2012年退休，並曾為傅爾布萊特基金、英國文化協會及數家大學的訪問學人。代表著作包括*Woman to Woman and Other Poems*（1997）、*Water Wood Pure Splendour*（2001）和*A Pond in the Sky*（2013），部分詩作並獲譯成德文、意大利文及其他語言。林舜玲於2008年獲愛荷華大學頒授寫作榮譽院士，並於意大利諾西德國際詩歌比賽奪得「特別表揚獎」。2009年，她榮獲香港民政事務局「嘉許狀」，以誌她於國際藝文活動的建樹。林舜玲致力學術研究，其著作*Language Education in China: Policy and Experience from 1949*（香港大學出版社，2005），論證新穎，領先同儕。近年她鑽研亞洲的英語詩作，備受矚目，其論著*Becoming Poets: The Asian English Experience*（Peter Lang, 2014）「參照之廣、探究之深」，實為「亞洲英語體驗的有力考察」（*Asiatic*，2015年12月號，書評人：Murari Prasad）。

Agnes S.L. Lam (Hong Kong) studied in Singapore and America. In 2012, she retired as Professor from the University of Hong Kong. She also held visitorships from Fulbright, the British Council and several universities at different times. Representative works include: *Woman to Woman and Other Poems* (1997), *Water Wood Pure Splendour* (2001) and *A Pond in the Sky* (2013). Some of her poems have been translated into German, Italian and other languages. An Honorary Fellow in Writing by the University of Iowa (2008), she was awarded the Nosside International Poetry Prize (Special Mention, 2008). In 2009, she also received a Commendation from the Home Affairs Bureau, HKSAR, in recognition of her outstanding achievements in international arts and cultural activities. As a researcher, she has long been well known for her pioneering volume, *Language Education in China: Policy and Experience from 1949* (HKU Press, 2005). More recently, she is also noted for her work on Asian poetry in English. Her book, *Becoming Poets: The Asian English Experience* (Peter Lang, 2014), "with its breadth of reference and depth of investigation," has been hailed as "a cogent assessment of the Asian English experience" (*Asiatic*, December 2015, reviewer: Murari Prasad).

香港國際詩歌之夜 2017
International Poetry Nights in Hong Kong 2017

主辦單位 Organizers

香港中文大學文學院
Faculty of Arts, The Chinese University of Hong Kong
香港詩歌節基金會有限公司
Hong Kong Poetry Festival Foundation Limited

協辦單位 Co-organizers

香港中文大學中國文化研究所
Institute of Chinese Studies, The Chinese University of Hong Kong
香港中文大學出版社
The Chinese University Press
香港大學美術博物館
The University Museum and Art Gallery, The University of Hong Kong
香港大學文學院
Faculty of Arts, The University of Hong Kong
香港科技大學賽馬會高等研究院
Jockey Club Institute for Advanced Study, Hong Kong University of Science and Technology
香港科技大學人文學部
Division of Humanities, Hong Kong University of Science and Technology
廣州時刻文化傳播有限公司
Moment Communications
活字文化
MoveableType Legacy (Beijing) Co., Ltd.
當當
DANGDANG

贊助 Sponsors

中國會 The China Club
北京匡時國際拍賣有限公司 Beijing Council International Auction Co., Ltd.
先鋒公益基金會 UCF Charity Foundation Limited
卓爾書店 the zall bookstore
斑馬谷文化發展有限公司 Zebra Valley Culture Development
馮鑫牟希文夫婦 Feng Xin (Larry) and Mu Xi Wen (Maggie)
蓮華書院 Lianhua Academy